Walther Ziegler

Marx
in 60 Minutes

Translated by
Alexander Reynolds

My thanks go to Rudolf Aichner for his tireless critical editing; Silke Ruthenberg for the fine graphics; Lydia Pointvogl, Eva Amberger, Christiane Hüttner, and Dr. Martin Engler for their excellent work as manuscript readers and sub-editors; Prof. Guntram Knapp, who first inspired me with enthusiasm for philosophy; and Angela Schumitz, who handled in the most professional manner, as chief editorial reader, the production of both the German and the English editions of this series of books.

My special thanks go to my translator

Dr Alexander Reynolds.

Himself a philosopher, he not only translated the original German text into English with great care and precision but also, in passages where this was required in order to ensure clear understanding, supplemented this text with certain formulations adapted specifically to the needs of English-language readers.

Bibliographic Information held by the German National Library: The details of the original German edition of this publication are held by the German National Library as part of the German National Bibliography; detailed bibliographical data can be found online at www.dnb.de.

© 2016 Dr Walther Ziegler
1st Edition June 2016
Jacket design and graphic design for the whole book: Silke Ruthenberg, making use of illustrations by:
Raphael Bräsecke, Creactive – Studio for Advertising, Comics & Illustrations
© JackF - Fotolia.com (image-frames)
© Valerie Potapova - Fotolia.com (image-frames)
© Svetlana Gryankina - Fotolia.com (speech-balloons)

Publisher and Printing:
BoD – Books on Demand, Norderstedt
ISBN 9783741227691

Contents

Marx's Great Discovery   7

Marx's Central Idea   14
   Man's Basic Material Needs   14
   Work   20
   Base and Superstructure   24
   Religion as 'the Opium of the People'   30
   History as Class Struggle   34
   The Theory of Surplus Value   45
   Accumulation and Concentration   48
   Immiseration and Revolution   54
   The "Withering Away of the State"   63
   Alienation   67
   Ending Alienation   70
   The Realm of Freedom   72

Of What Use Is Marx's Discovery for Us Today?   74
   Beware of the Sorceror –
   How Can Man Maintain Control?   74
   Every Era Has Its Ideology, Even Our Own –
   The "Critique of Ideology" Today   80

Making the „Realm of Freedom" a Reality – Work is Just a Staging Post	87
Egoism May Bring Success – But Man Finds Completion Only as a "Species-Being"	92
Bibliographical References	**97**

Marx's Great Discovery

The philosophical effort undertaken by Marx (1818-1883) was an enormous one. He was the first to attempt to decipher the law of motion of the whole of human history. He wanted to draw from the course of history prior to his own day certain precise insights about future developments, so that this history could be guided in a more rational direction.

Such an enterprise appears at first sight impossible, even megalomaniac. How can a human being – even a philosopher, however wise and far-sighted – predict the future, let alone hope to exert an influence on future historical developments?

But Karl Marx did in fact succeed in drawing philosophical, economic and socio-political conclusions from past and present events which were, in later years, really borne out in many nations. Some hundred years after his death a third of the human race was living in states whose social systems bore Marx's name. In the course of the last century, "Marxism" spread across the entire world. Never before or since has an individual philosopher had such a huge effect.

Social conditions in Marx's own lifetime – particularly the working conditions in the newly-emerged factories – were catastrophic. Not just men, but women and children too, had to work twelve to fourteen hours a day and the living conditions and hygiene levels in the slums these workers lived in were an offence to human dignity. Marx considered it his duty to take the part of those who were suffering in this way and to bring about revolutionary change.

But Marx was of the view that it was not just his task but that of all philosophers to work toward the improvement of society. Philosophers, he argued, should no longer, as they had for two thousand years, be content with understanding and interpreting the world. Writing on the near-contemporary philosopher Feuerbach, Marx declared:

The philosophers have only *interpreted* the world in various ways; the point is to *change* it. ²

Thus, the young Marx observed, for several years, as a journalist and philosopher, the day-to-day politics, history, and economic development of Europe until he believed he had gained an understanding of the causes of all these processes. Humanity's whole development, he concluded, from antiquity right up to the present day, consisted in a necessary sequence of great conflicts between different social groupings:

The history of all hitherto existing society is the history of class struggles. [3]

There occur, Marx argued, at regular intervals great revolutions which radically alter the way in which society is ruled and, with this, its economic foundations. Marx himself, along with his family, lived through just such a time of revolutions. He supported, in his newspaper articles, Germany's revolution of 1848, composing in this year, together with his friend Engels, the famous *Communist Manifesto*.

This call to revolution earned him the bitter enmity of the Prussian king, then ruler of Marx's native Rhineland. Deprived of his nationality and in danger of arrest, he was forced to flee across the border to France. But the Prussian king pursued him even there, demanding his extradition, so that he finally had no choice but to take his family into permanent exile in England. There too, however, he continued to work on his revolutionary writings.

However, the money that he earned from his newspaper articles and his books was not enough to feed his family of six. In a letter to his friend Engels (who helped him with sums of money sent from Germany) dated 8th of September 1852 he wrote:

> My wife is ill, little Jenny is ill, little Lene has a kind of nervous fever. I could not and cannot call the doctor because I have no money for medicine. For 8-10 days I have kept the family going on bread and potatoes, and today it is even doubtful whether I can get these. [4]

Marx, then, had bitter personal experience of the poverty he denounced. He lived through the process of Europe's industrialization and saw how, all around him, cities grew at an astonishing rate and how more and more people flooded from the country into the great metropolises to work day and night in the factories. He saw how children were made to produce, for starvation wages, huge masses of fabric at the machines of the textile factories. And he saw how railways rapidly joined up all the cities of Europe, how mines were dug in their thousands, and how steamships full of a million wares began to ply the ocean between Europe and America.

Marx analysed, with fascination, this rapidly progressing industrialization and came to the conclusion that the modern capitalist mode of production meant that incomparably more goods could now be produced than ever before in history – but also that the great majority of the human race remained excluded from the wealth and prosperity so created. He was also firmly convinced that the free play of supply and demand would, in the long term, collapse and lead to global crises. This was why he criticized the capitalist system and recommended the abolition of private property. In its place he proposed putting a new kind of collective mode of production: so-called "communism".

The effects of these ideas were enormous. Communist revolutions occurred in countries as diverse as Russia, China, Cuba, Nicaragua, and Mozambique, as well as many others. For almost a whole century, communist and socialist regimes declared themselves adherents to the historical and social philosophy of Marx.

But the planned economies favoured by these states proved to be clumsy and, in many areas, inefficient. Around a hundred years after Marx's death the communist world that he had called into existence had largely vanished again. Since the dissolution of the Soviet Union in the 1990s, communism is considered by most to be a failed project. After the fall of the Iron Curtain many were of the view that Marx had simply been wrong and that capitalism is in fact the only economic system apt to bring prosperity. It was hoped that a market economy could exist in harmony with democracy and a fair distribution of wealth. But this optimism did not last long.

The global economic and financial crises of the last few decades have deeply shaken this faith in capitalism's ability to regulate itself. It is becoming ever clearer that capitalism too has its structural weaknesses.

Some of Marx's predictions – such as increasing monopolization and an ever greater global gap between rich and poor – have already come true, while others are taking form on the historical horizon. His insightful critique of capitalism, then, is more relevant than ever. Marx surely still has a lot to say to us.

Marx's Central Idea

Man's Basic Material Needs

Marx's philosophical starting point is of appealing simplicity, and basically uncontestable. Every human being needs food and drink. To be without these for a long time is to die. Marx writes:

Life involves, before everything else, eating and drinking, housing and clothing, and various other things. [5]

This is why every philosophy must take these basic material needs as its point of departure. It makes no sense, Marx argues, to begin a philosophical theory with thoughts about God, justice, or even human reason, since none of these things would be possible without the taking of nourishment, that is, direct material exchange with Nature. For Marx, therefore, there stands at the beginning of philosophy, and of human history, the simple fact that Man must work in order to satisfy his material needs:

> The first historical act is thus the production of the means to satisfy these needs, the production of material life itself [...]. ⁶

This initial historical act of the production of the means of existence is one which we continue to perform even today. Because a caveman breaking open a nutshell with a stone to get at the nut, a farmer using a tractor to bring in his crop, or a molecular biologist using genetic engineering to increase future crop yields are all instances of Man acquiring something from Nature or, as Marx puts it, "appropriating Nature":

> All production is appropriation of Nature [...]. ⁷

Man, then, is not, primarily, anything spiritual or divine. His needs, Marx argues, are above all material. Just like an animal, Man appropriates the material things he needs. However, there is a decisive difference which sets human beings, at a certain point in their evolution, off from other animals:

They themselves begin to distinguish themselves from animals as soon as they begin to *produce* their means of subsistence [...]. [8]

An animal does not actually produce its means of subsistence. It finds its nourishment directly in Nature and can consume it directly without help of any sort. The buffalo simply eats the grass on the plain. And even predatory animals that hunt down their sources of food remain, in their life-activity, in harmony with inner and outer Nature:

Marx's Central Idea

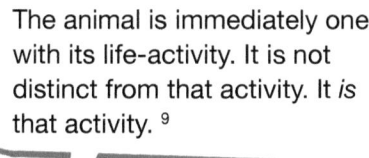

> The animal is immediately one with its life-activity. It is not distinct from that activity. It *is* that activity. [9]

In Man's case the process of appropriating Nature is much more complex, ramified and comprehensive. The farmer produces the means of subsistence, but someone else the fertilizer, yet a third person the machines with which the harvest is brought in, a fourth the fuel for the farmer's tractor and for the other machines. A fifth person builds the refinery which manufactures the diesel oil; a sixth runs the fleet of tankers which transport this oil; a seventh makes the headframes at the wells. And all this is only the beginning. In fact, a very long series of work-steps is required for the farmer to harvest his wheat and just as long a series before bread can be baked from it and be laid out, packed, on supermarket shelves.

In contrast to animals, then, Man survives only through the division and specialization of labour. Indeed, even once they are in the supermarket, people cannot simply take products off the shelves but must have earned the money to pay for them:

Labour, therefore, [is] a necessary condition, independent of all forms of society, for the existence of the human race. It is an eternal, Nature-imposed necessity, without which there can be no material exchanges between Man and Nature, and therefore no life. 10

Here one might object that animals too must work for their food and shelter. Do beavers not build dams in order to regulate the water level in front of their lodges? But Marx had already asked himself this question:

Marx's Central Idea

> It is true that animals also produce. They build nests and dwellings, like the bee, the beavers, the ant etc. But they produce only their own immediate needs or those of their young. They produce one-sidedly, whilst Man produces universally. [11]

Man's universal production is indeed impressive. Today there are more than 14,000 different professions by which human beings earn their living. Ant and bee colonies have, indeed, their "workers", "sentinels" and "queens". But a division and specialization of labour as complex and ramified as that of human beings is found nowhere in the animal kingdom.

Work

Man, then, must work in order to satisfy his basic needs for food, clothing and shelter. Once we have firmly grasped this simple fact we have understood Marx's central philosophical idea. Because the notion of work – and of the securing, through work, of basic needs – forms the foundation for Marx's whole philosophy of dialectical materialism.

> The practical creation of an *objective world* by his personal activity, the *fashioning* of inorganic Nature, is proof that Man is a conscious species-being[...]. [12]

For Marx, then, Man proves and realizes his own being through the process of work, which means in turn that this being is essentially a species-being, that is to say, a being-in-community with others. For in fact it is only very exceptionally that a human being works alone. Mostly, work is done together with colleagues, be it in an office, on a building site, or in a factory. Even in seemingly one-man professions, one remains a species-being dependent on others: the artist may be alone in his studio, but he produces his works for others, sells them to them, and then himself buys food and clothes from the profits. Thus, everyone is bound into society right from the cradle on. Marx stresses how an individual is marked and formed in his deepest nature by his parents, his schooling, and above all by the work he does. For this reason, Marx goes so far as to call the individual human being the totality, or concrete co-presence, of the social relationships that make him up:

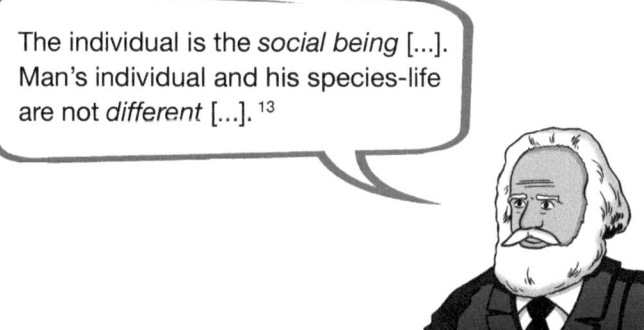

> The individual is the *social being* [...]. Man's individual and his species-life are not *different* [...]. [13]

The way that a human being works within his society plays a decisive role in forming his self-awareness.

A Tibetan monk, for example, who earns his livelihood tending vegetables in the monastery garden has a completely different awareness of himself than does a worker in a steel works, or someone caring for children in a kindergarten, a bank manager, a professional footballer, a musician, or a butcher. The work we do forms us:

> By producing their means of subsistence men are indirectly producing their material life [...]. As individuals express their life, so they are. [14]

Marx is really saying something very simple here, namely: we are what we do and how we do it. The way in which we earn our living plays such a decisive role because work directly determines human beings' feeling and thinking:

> What (human beings) are, therefore, coincides with their production: both with what they produce and with *how* they produce. [15]

By this Marx means not only how an individual produces but also how his whole society does. Thus, the warlike Vikings, for example, who earned their livelihood by daring raids and brutal assaults, had an entirely different sense of themselves than did, for example, nations composed of farmers who lived by the patient and careful cultivation of the fields. Marx, indeed, goes a step further and says that absolutely everything that occurs in people's minds – their deepest convictions, their morality, and even their religion – are always only reflections of the material relations of production in which people live. In Marx's own terminology, all ideas are nothing but a mental "superstructure" resting on their respective material "base".

Base and Superstructure

This theory of base and superstructure is of central importance in Marx's materialist philosophy. All that is "mental" – i.e. the apparently free thoughts of individuals and "consciousness" with its many plans and intentions – are, for Marx, only reflections of material circumstances. Here he directly contradicts the great German philosopher Hegel, who always emphasized the mental and spiritual development of Man. This, Marx argued, had been Hegel's fundamental error. It is not consciousness and its decisions that determine our lives; on the contrary, it is material life that determines what takes place in our heads. This materialist reversal of Hegel's view is the deeper meaning of the oft-cited Marxist dictum: 'being determines consciousness'. Marx's actual words in this passage are:

> Hence, what individuals are depends on the material conditions of their production. [...] It is not consciousness that determines life but life that determines consciousness. [16]

Thus, human societies have passed, in the course of history, through different forms of production which have, in their turn, given rise to different religious and artistic currents as "superstructures" to these material "bases". The basis of everything, however, always remains the mode of production:

> Religion, the family, the state, law, morality, science, art etc. are only *particular* modes of production [...]. [17]

The example of the Vikings can help us to understand why, for Marx, even religion is just an after-effect of social production. So-called "predatory" nations like the Vikings gain the greater part of what they live on by attacks and raids; the god that they worship above all other gods is generally a brave and aggressive god of war. But nations whose livelihood is based on agriculture tend to celebrate harvest festivals and revere a god associated with the weather. The worship of a thunder god or a sun god who can be asked not to ruin the harvest but let it grow and ripen is,

Marx claims, just the necessary superstructure to the material basis of a nation of farmers sustaining their lives through agriculture, whose very survival depends on what the harvest yields. Nations living by the sea, however, who live by fishing or maritime trade, tend to worship gods associated with the wind or the tides. Mining nations have worshipped Saint Barbara, patron saint of mining. Sedentary nations build temples on the hills above their fields, while nomadic peoples, driving their herds before them, may carry the temple of their god with them in something like the ancient Jewish "ark of the covenant". Thus, in each case, the material base determines the specific ceremonies and substance of the religion.

Smaller nations can afford to worship many gods but great empires, like Rome, eventually require, if they are not to be split apart by a hundred different cults, a single god who will link and reconcile all the smaller deities. The Emperor Constantine's abolition of polytheism and introduction of monotheistic Christianity was also a case of the necessary emergence of a superstructure appropriate to Rome's vast material base. Marx's best friend, Friedrich Engels, sums up the base / superstructure theory succinctly: "[...] we can only draw the one conclusion: that men, consciously or unconsciously, derive their ethical ideas in the last resort from the practical relations [...] in which they carry on production and exchange." [18]

This was why Marx and Engels developed their own "matter"-focussed philosophy specifically as a critique of the purely "idea"-focussed philosophy that dominated Germany in their youth:

In direct contrast to German philosophy, which descends from heaven to earth, here it is a matter of ascending from earth to heaven. That is to say, of not setting out from what men say, imagine, or conceive [...]. [19]

The German philosophy referred to here (that of Fichte, Schelling and Hegel) set out, Marx held, from these men's personal ideas of God. Marx's materialist philosophy set out from an opposite starting point:

> (It sets out) from real, active men and, on the basis of their real life-process (demonstrates) the development of the ideological reflections and echoes of this life-process. [20]

By ideological reflections and echoes Marx means not only the direct reflection of a society's conditions of work in its religion. He also proposes the thesis that the mode of production of any class society will tend to create a consciousness in the minds of that society's dominated class which excuses and justifies the domination it suffers. Thus, for example, under feudalism it was very important that serfs and landless peasants all believed that their feudal lords had "blue blood" and that God had appointed these lords to rule just as He had appointed the serfs and peasants to serve and be ruled. This worldview of "divine rights" absolved kings and noblemen of any need to explain or justify their living from the taxes and tributes of the peasants without doing any work themselves. What Marx called "ideology" is simply "false consciousness" inasmuch as the ideas and beliefs concerned do not serve the population as a whole but only a small part of it. The superstructure reflects always only the consciousness of the class that rules the society in question, never that of the ruled:

Religion as 'the Opium of the People'

> Man makes religion; religion does not make Man. [22]

Of all the shared mental phenomena that make up what he calls the superstructure it is religion that Marx criticizes the most. For down the centuries religion has always possessed a special importance.

> Religion is the general theory of this world, [...] its solemn complement, and its universal basis of consolation and justification [...]. Religion is only the illusory sun which revolves around Man as long as he does not revolve around himself. [23]

Religion, says Marx, has the function of consoling mankind inasmuch as it explains and justifies the many sufferings that must be borne in life. Religion promises Man an afterlife in Paradise as compensation for all the injustice and torment we undergo in the "here below". Marx compares this pacifying effect of religion with the effect of a drug:

Religion is the sigh of the oppressed creature. [...] It is the *opium* of the people. [24]

The prospect of a happy afterlife in the "world above" may indeed have the benefit of consolation. But this benefit is also religion's great drawback: it dissuades from the attempt to improve the "here below". This is why Marx demands religion's abolition:

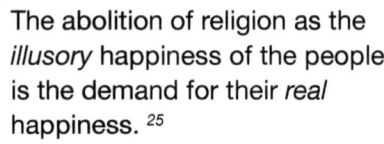

"The abolition of religion as the *illusory* happiness of the people is the demand for their *real* happiness." [25]

Religion must be critiqued at every possible turn because (so Marx hoped) if we succeed in abolishing it energies will be set free which can be applied to tackling and solving the real problems of Man's life on earth:

"Thus, the criticism of heaven turns into the criticism of the earth." [26]

As long as God continues to be thought of by Man as the Supreme Being, every injustice can be justified by calling it a "test from God":

Marx's Central Idea

> The criticism of religion ends with the teaching that for *Man the Supreme Being is Man*, and thus with the *Categorical Imperative to overthrow all relations* in which Man is a debased, enslaved, abandoned, despicable being [...]. [27]

This passage expresses the core idea of Marx's whole philosophy. All material conditions and relations must be overthrown under which Man remains an enslaved being.

History as Class Struggle

For Marx, history is nothing other than the succession of different phases of material production. At the dawn of history human beings produced their means of subsistence collectively. They lived together in hordes and tribes. Tribal – or, as Marx and Engels sometimes call it, "gentile" – society is concerned above all with the survival of the tribe: "Production at all previous stages of society was essentially common production, and likewise consumption took place by the direct distribution of the products within larger or smaller communistic communities." [28]

Thus, for example, North American Indians went as a tribe on their buffalo hunts and then divided the meat up among all the tribespeople. These early tribal societies were classless social structures in which there existed no private property, and thus no "haves" nor "have-nots". Everything belonged to everyone. It would, indeed, have made no sense to amass private property. When an Indian tribe, for example, broke camp in order to follow the herd of buffalo, nothing could be taken along that could not be easily carried. It was pointless to accumulate "luxury" goods, beyond a few plates and bowls. There was also not yet any division of labour nor any money. Thus every Indian was able to manufacture all he needed – from his bow and arrow to the poles of his tent – himself. Engels describes the way such early tribal societies reproduced themselves as unselfish and healthy: "As long as production was carried on on this basis, it could not grow beyond the control of the producers and it could not conjure up any alien, phantom powers against them, as is the case regularly and inevitably under civilization." [29]

Marx and Engels do not describe this classless primitive state in much detail. But they do point out that this early tribal society did not need private property to materially sustain itself. Indeed, property relations were not a marked feature of early tribal cultures. We know from the descriptions of the Roman historian Tacitus that it was the custom of the ancient Germanic tribes to send half of their male members to war while the other half stayed to tend the fields with the womenfolk (the man who had stayed behind one year going to war the next).

It was only, Marx argued, as agriculture progressed and there occurred a general transition from nomadic to sedentary ways of life that the first societies characterized by private property - above all the "human property" of slaves- took shape. Marx and Engels make a distinction here between Asiatic and European slave-owning societies (i.e. the Persian and the Roman forms of despotism). It is from this point on that all further historical development is characterized by conflicts between ruling groups and ruled: so-called "classes".

> The history of all hitherto existing society is the history of class struggles. [30]

But this conflict between the classes is the motor that drives history on:

> Freeman and slave, patrician and plebeian, lord and serf, guild-master and journeyman, in a word, oppressor and oppressed, stood in constant

> opposition to one another, carried on an uninterrupted fight, a fight that each time ended [...] in a revolutionary reconstitution of society at large [...]. [31]

Upon slavery-based society there followed feudal society which was also marked by its characteristic conflict. Because all the nobility of this society, and even the king himself, lived, in the last analysis, entirely off of what was produced by the peasants, tradesmen, merchants and citizens who held their land and livelihoods only by feudal tenure. The nobility of this epoch looked on labour as an ignoble pursuit. They carried parasols so as to be distinguishable at a glance from the sunburnt field-labourers and also rejected all commercial activity as beneath the dignity of their class. But this inclination of the noble class to leave such activities as trade and banking entirely in the hands of others created a new class of special confidence and self-awareness: the town-dwelling "burghers", or so-called "bourgeoisie". While the nobles were satisfied just to govern their vast rural domains and live off the taxes and corvée labour extracted from their serfs, this bourgeoisie founded, in their towns and cities, tradesmen's workshops and even rudimentary factories. Very soon, this new class was generating, on their tiny urban areas of land, much more wealth than the nobility could generate on all its vast rural domains. The noble class all over Europe became indebted to this new class of tradesmen, manufacturers and merchant bankers. And the poorer the nobles became through their debts to the urban bourgeoisie, the richer this new urban class grew. At a certain point they demanded a political power in keeping with their economic one until all Europe was shaken by "bourgeois revolutions" and feudalism, along with its whole cultural "superstructure", collapsed.

But just as the feudal nobility had raised up its own successor, the bourgeoisie, by leaving to this latter all trade and commerce, this new bourgeois ruling class likewise created and raised up a successor of its own, or its "dialectical negation", as Marx put it. In this context "dialectic" means simply that the ruling class brings forth an oppressed class, which leads to further class struggle out of which there emerges yet another new form of society.

The collapse of feudal society and the seizing of power by the bourgeoisie leads to an enormous increase in material production:

> The bourgeoisie, during its rule of scarce one hundred years, has created more massive and more colossal productive forces than have all preceding generations together. [32]

Already at this time, says Marx, there begins an unstoppable process of globalization:

> In place of the old local and national seclusion and self-sufficiency, we have intercourse in every direction, universal interdependence of nations. [33]

In contrast to tribal, slave-based, and feudal societies which had been sustained almost solely by agricultural production, production is now primarily industrial. And this new mode of production dramatically alters the whole world:

> Subjection of Nature's forces to Man, machinery, application of chemistry to industry and agriculture, steam navigation, railways, electric telegraphs, clearing of whole continents for cultivation, canalization of rivers, whole populations conjured out of the ground – what earlier century had even a presentiment that such productive forces slumbered in the lap of social labour? [34]

But as Marx points out, the wealth which results from these enormous new achievements in the sphere of production is not shared in by all members of the new society. On the contrary, it is the bourgeoisie alone that owns all the means of production, from the machines down to the great wholesale warehouses from which the produced goods are sold. The workers, on the other hand, and all those who depend on wages, own nothing but their own ability to work (or "labour-power", as Marx terms it). Here as well, then, two necessarily hostile classes confront each other: the bourgeoisie and the workers, or "proletariat".

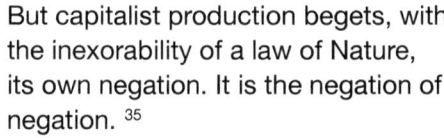

But capitalist production begets, with the inexorability of a law of Nature, its own negation. It is the negation of negation. [35]

Since the bourgeoisie had already represented the historical antagonist – or, phrased in the more abstract philosophical terminology that Marx took over from Hegel, the "negation" – of the feudal nobility, the proletariat can logically be called the "negation of negation". Because this new ruling class once again creates, in the form of the ever less adequately paid working class, its own antagonist. In one of the most famous passages of their *Communist Manifesto* Marx and Engels exhort this working class to seize power:

> The proletarians have nothing to lose but their chains. They have a world to win. Working men of all countries, unite! [36]

It is Marx's contention that a proletarian revolution will mean a final dissolving of all class antagonisms, since the proletariat, once it has achieved common ownership of the means of production, will simply dissolve as a separate class.

This model of history developed by Marx is basically a very simple one. It starts with a kind of "primitive communism" because early tribal societies were classless and propertyless societies where everyone hunted and tended the fields together. But through the division of labour and the development of technology there arose – with the slave-based societies of antiquity, feudal societies, and then our own society dominated by the bourgeoisie – a series of societies wherein private property made people "alienated" from their own working lives. In the end, though, Marx sees private property being abolished again by the communist revolution and the original classless society being re-established.

The final goal of history, then, is the unity of individual and society and reconciliation of class with class. For Marx and Engels, achieving this is a task that falls specifically to the working class which, at the highest point of capitalist expansion, takes political power and establishes a just society in which no one is any longer the slave of anyone else. But this does not occur because the workers suddenly have the idea of making a revolution. To think this would be once again to practice a mere "philosophy of ideas". For Marx, on the contrary, it is the material relations of production themselves that come into contradiction with one another and cause capitalism to collapse like a house of cards. It is in his legendary main work, *Das Kapital*, that Marx shows how these forces internal to capitalism come into contradiction with one another. The core of this work is formed by theories of surplus value, accumulation, concentration, and immiseration – all of them as relevant still today as when they were formulated.

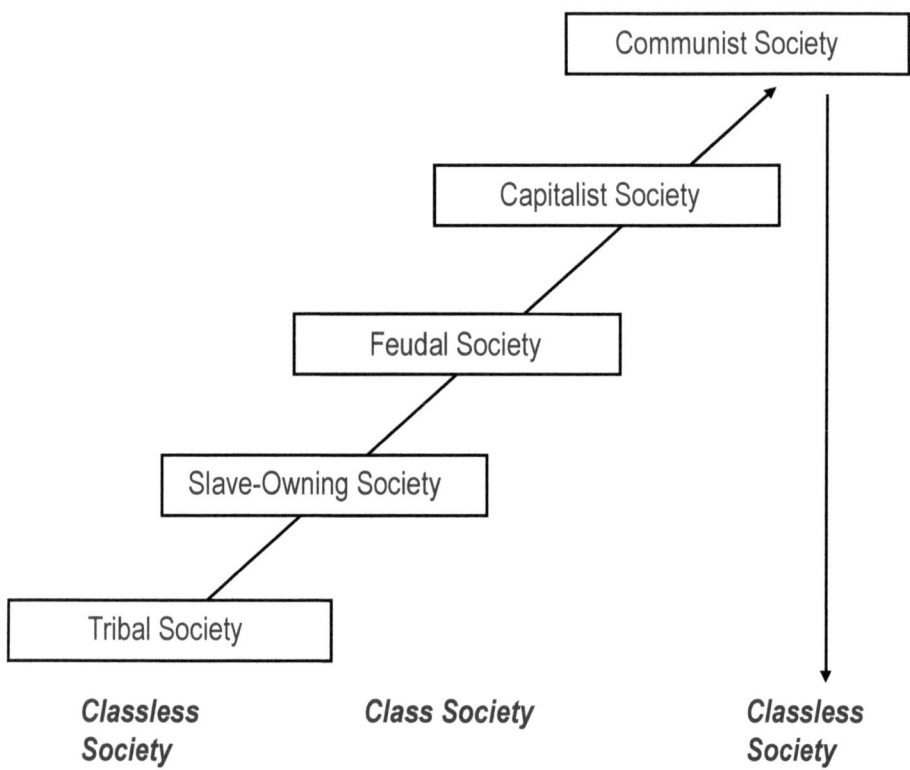

The Theory of Surplus Value

The capitalist does not pay the worker all the value that the worker creates for him. He pays him a sum significantly smaller than this and keeps for himself the "surplus value" produced by the work performed. Marx gives examples here of factories in which workers are paid directly in the form of food, distributed in amounts that are just sufficient to sustain them and their families. All money in excess of this – acquired by the sale of the goods produced and thereby, ultimately, through the work of the workers – is retained by the capitalist:

> The worker receives means of subsistence in exchange for his labour-power; but the capitalist receives, in exchange for his means of subsistence, labour, [...] the creative power by which the worker not only replaces what he consumes but gives to the accumulated labour a greater value than it previously possessed. [37]

Let us assume that a worker produces, during a 12-hour shift in a cotton mill, enough cotton to make shirts and trousers with a final sales value of 1000 pounds. But the factory-owner pays him, for the 12 hours of work performed, only 60 pounds. The owner's other costs – in terms of paying off the loans used to buy the factory premises and the machines, the wages of the gateman, the book-keeper and the cleaners, and the price of raw cotton being worked – amount to 30 pounds per worker per day. There remains, then, for the capitalist, once the work-wages of 60 pounds have been paid out and these further costs covered, a "surplus value" of 910 pounds. The factory-owner's capital will thus rapidly increase. This is why Marx poses the rhetorical question:

Does a worker in a cotton factory produce merely cotton textiles? No. He produces capital. [38]

Because the worker sells not his specific acts of labour but rather his labour-power he loses all claim upon the product which his labour produces. Even if this product, in the end, proves to possess a very high use-value and is sold at a correspondingly high market price, the worker receives in exchange for his labour-power only its initially agreed value, as a mere expenditure of time, in the form of an hourly wage-rate.

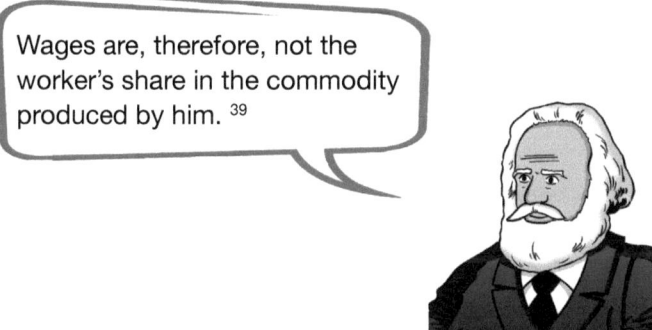

Wages are, therefore, not the worker's share in the commodity produced by him. [39]

On the contrary, the worker's hourly wage amounts as a rule to far less than the value that he actually produces within that hour. It is the factory-owner alone who gains from the high price brought by that product which is, in fact, a result of the worker's labouring activity. The factory-owner, for a day or longer, "makes use" of the worker's labour-power in order to incorporate this value-creating labour-power into a product that would otherwise be lifeless. The "surplus value" that is added to the product is thereby a value that the factory-owner retains for himself alone, thereby becoming ever wealthier.

Accumulation and Concentration

The surplus value so generated is invested again by the capitalist factory-owner and leads in turn to the production of still more surplus value. Capital thus automatically creates still greater capital.

Production of surplus value is the absolute law of this mode of production. [40]

Once this process has begun it cannot be halted. Each capitalist enterprise is obliged to continue to grow, to increase its production, and to open up new markets for its goods. If such an enterprise were to choose restraint and forego such constant expansion, it would be running the risk of being pushed out of the market by larger enterprises. Consequently, each enterprise is compelled always to increase its strength of capital by re-investing profits in order to generate still greater profits.

But once all potential areas for sales have been opened up, and the markets thus opened have been saturated, the only way left for a capitalist enterprise to expand is for it to take over – or to buy up, swallow, or otherwise destroy – the production facilities of other such enterprises. A capitalist enterprise that fails to do this risks being swallowed up itself; whoever does not expand is eliminated. Therefore, Marx contends, every capitalist must always be trying to defeat all his competitors and to drive them from the market. In this war of pitiless competition the capitalist tends to use above all one proven weapon:

The battle of competition is fought by cheapening of commodities. [41]

A capitalist who hopes to monopolize the market for screwdrivers needs, in order to do so, only to offer his screwdrivers, for a period, at a significantly lower price than his competitors. If he succeeds in clearly undercutting the prices of another manufacturer for a long stretch of time, this other manufacturer will no longer be able to sell his comparatively expensive products on the market. Sooner or later he will either have to cease production or sell his enterprise to the larger capitalist. What is decisive, then, for survival under conditions of capitalist competition is price:

The cheapness of commodities depends [...] upon the productiveness of labour, and this again upon the scale of production. Therefore, the larger capitals beat the smaller. [42]

Thus, the process of capital accumulation and that of capital concentration are closely bound up with one another. The capitalist with the greater amount of capital, being able to achieve a higher rate of accu-

Marx's Central Idea

mulation, can, in the long term, amass significantly more capital and use it to force his competitors to their knees by selling his goods at artificially low prices. He has, so to speak, a greater financial "stamina" and can afford to bear losses for a period of time if this allows him to ruin some competitor he wants out of the way:

Competition [...] always ends in the ruin of many small capitalists whose capitals partly pass into the hands of their conquerors, partly vanish. [43]

Once, however, a company producing a product has succeeded in dominating the market and has become, for example, one of the few or even the sole provider of electrical power, this company can demand for this power whatever price it wishes, since it has no competitors. Millions of consumers are then dependent upon this sole surviving producer. The next step is for the monopolist to use his capital – which now accumulates still more rapidly – to open up new branches of business for himself and to move toward monopolizing still more markets. In this way capitalist production creates a new field of forces upon which the whole of society becomes henceforth entirely dependent, namely, the system of banking and credit institutions:

[...] With capitalist production an altogether new force comes into play: the credit system. [...] By unseen threads [...] it draws the disposable money, scattered in larger or smaller masses over the surface of society, into the hands of individual or associated capitalists. It is the specific machine for the centralization of capitals. 44

Marx's Central Idea

Due to the takeovers and mergers that ensue from capitalist competition more and more small capitalists come to be expropriated by larger ones. The few very large capitalist enterprises that survive mercilessly push on the process of monopoly-formation through their struggle to dominate the global market:

One capitalist always kills many. Hand in hand with this centralization, or this expropriation of many capitalists by few, develop [...] the conscious technical application of science, the methodical cultivation of the soil, [...] the entanglement of all peoples in the net of the world market, and with this the international character of the capitalistic regime. [45]

Immiseration and Revolution

The direct consequence, in turn, of capital accumulation and concentration is the immiseration of the mass of the people. As a small number of globally operating enterprises concentrate ever more capital within themselves – i.e. basically, become richer and richer – this money proves lacking in other areas of society. Eventually, a world arises in which massive amounts of wealth accumulate in the hands of the heads of these giant corporations while workers, normal citizens and consumers suffer greater and greater destitution:

> Capital grows in one place to a huge mass in a single hand because it has in another place been lost by many. [46]

For as long as there still exist many small enterprises the market functions well. But as soon as the process of capital concentration brings it about that just a few huge concerns seize control of the production of all goods, all equilibrium is lost and immiseration begins:

> Along with the constantly diminishing number of the magnates of capital [...] (there) grows the mass of misery, oppression, slavery, degradation, exploitation; but with this too grows the revolt of the working class, a class always increasing in numbers. [47]

No individual capitalist entrepreneur can be said to be personally guilty here of driving workers into poverty. Each such entrepreneur is simply complying, after all, with the laws of competition in a market economy and is obliged to think in business-economic terms. If he is not to be undercut in the ongoing price war by some other company and driven into insolvency, he must try to lower costs and raise his profit rate. He pays, then, the lowest salaries possible, transfers his production abroad, replaces workers with machines and cuts back on administrative staff. In this way he significantly lowers his wages bill and is able to produce his goods more cheaply. But the consequence of all this is a further drop in the purchasing power of the workers and other employees that the entrepreneur has replaced with machines and driven into unemployment. Since it is not just him but also other entrepreneurs in other branches of production that are acting in this way, more and more workers are either employed at very low wages or laid off altogether. But a population sinking ever deeper into poverty cannot buy or consume goods, so that the profits of the goods-producing entrepreneurs sink still further, which obliges the entrepreneur in his turn to impose shorter working hours or more layoffs. The downward spiral, then, continues and immiseration increases. Products pile up in the warehouses while more and more unemployed wait in vain at factory gates for work:

> The greater the social wealth, the functioning capital, the extent and energy of its growth [...] the greater is the industrial reserve army. [48]

In order to break out of this economic vicious circle of insufficient purchasing power leading to further falls in production, the entrepreneurs would have to offer voluntarily, together and all at once, higher wages to all their workers, so that these latter could begin to buy goods once again.

The entrepreneurs, however, would never do such a thing. An entrepreneur must always think in terms of the advantage of his own enterprise rather than that of the economy as a whole. So long as his sales continue to fall, then, such an entrepreneur will continue to lay off workers and the economic crisis deepens and spreads worldwide, leading to recession and mass unemployment. At a certain point barely any products are sold at all any more. Capitalism, argues Marx, sinks, under the pressure of its own measures of "rationalization", so deeply into recession that many firms close down altogether and all their workers join the ranks of the unemployed.

In the end a great army of jobless people waits before the closed gates of factories full of machines that nobody operates; nobody operates these machines because the products they produce are not sold; and the products are not sold precisely because those who might have bought them are waiting, uselessly, before the gates of the production facilities. This moment – at which human social production has become a vicious circle of non-production – is, for Marx, the moment of revolution:

At a certain stage of development the material productive forces of society come into conflict with the existing relations of production [...]. [49]

By "material productive forces" here Marx means the workers and the entrepreneurs; by "existing relations of production" he means the machines, the factories and the way in which production is carried on. The "conflict" he refers to consists simply in the facts that, as the global economy slips into crisis, a few owners and entrepreneurs of technologically well-equipped firms find themselves face to face with many unemployed people without purchasing power, and that, since the latter are unable to buy any goods, the former are unable to produce any. When the system has crippled itself so completely, the workers them-

Marx's Central Idea

selves, in a revolutionary act, take over the machinery of production. They expropriate those monopoly capitalists who have already swallowed up into their huge capitalist concerns all the smaller capitalists. It is the hour, as Marx puts it, of the "expropriation of the expropriators":

Centralization of the means of production and socialization of labour at last reach a point where they become incompatible with their capitalist integument. This integument is burst asunder. [...] The expropriators are expropriated. [50]

It is important to note here that Marx sees the revolution as coming about due to a real contradiction inherent in the material facts and not simply because some worker, or Marx himself, had the idea of having a revolution. Capitalism, so to speak, abolishes itself by entangling itself in material self-contradictions. The communism that now follows is likewise just the material result of this historical development. Marx and Engels lay great emphasis on this:

Communism is not, for us, a *state of affairs* which is to be established, an *ideal* to which reality [will] have to adjust itself. [51]

Communism is rather a material movement which emerges from the real internal contradictions of capitalism. Marx and Engels are materialists. This is why they repeatedly stress that the revolution cannot be the result of an idea and certainly not the result of their own philosophy but must proceed solely out of the process of material development:

> The theoretical conclusions of the communists are in no way based on ideas or principles that have been invented [...] They merely express, in general terms, actual relations springing from an existing class struggle [...]. ⁵²

These "actual relations" in which workers lived in Marx's day certainly were, in many states, inhumane and degrading and spurred workers on to struggle for better living conditions. The workers' districts had neither proper lighting nor sewerage. The vote was restricted to wealthier, property-owning citizens. Marx's contemporary Ferdinand Lassalle, the worker's leader and founder of the party that was later to become the Social Democrats, considered this issue, above all, to be central. He called for universal suffrage, hoping that workers, once they could send their own representatives to parliament, would achieve a shortening of the working day and other rights by passing laws to this effect. Marx, for his part, was much more sceptical about the workers' seizing power by the peaceful, parliamentary path:

This issue became a point of bitter contention between Marx and Lassalle. Marx argued that Lassalle's proto-social-democratic political line would delay rather than hasten the necessary seizure of the means of production by the working class, since it would encourage workers to be satisfied with just small concessions from the side of the capitalist class and their government. For Marx, it was a full revolution, and this alone, that was needed:

Marx's Central Idea

> Both for the production on a mass scale of [...] communist consciousness and for the success of the cause itself the alteration of men on a mass scale is necessary – an alteration which can only take place in a practical movement, a *revolution*. [54]

The "Withering Away of the State"

Marx and Engels were also convinced that the whole superstructure – for example, the legal system which refused to workers the right to vote – could only be toppled once a clean and fundamental break had been made:

> [...] the revolution is necessary [...] not only because the *ruling* class cannot be overthrown in any other way but

> also because the class *overthrowing* it can only in a revolution succeed in ridding itself of all the muck of ages and become fitted to found society anew. [55]

In another passage, however, Marx speaks not of a single great revolution but rather of an "era of social revolution", which would suggest a process of overturning more differentiated and spread out over space and time:

> Then begins an era of social revolution. The changes in the economic foundation lead sooner or later to the transformation of the whole immense superstructure. [56]

In that transitional phase which is that of the revolution itself, say Marx and Engels, there may emerge a "dictatorship of the proletariat" – but only for as long as it takes to transfer all machines, factories and large-scale agricultural enterprises into social ownership. Bourgeois private property is abolished. Everyone works henceforth in enterprises collectively owned by the people. But as soon as the process of transformation is completed the coercion which the proletariat is obliged to exert during this transitional phase is no longer necessary. "Government" in the classical sense with its power of domination over human beings is gradually replaced by the mere administration of the collectively-owned production centres. The state as an instrument of the ruling class spontaneously "withers away" and in its place there emerges what Marx calls a free "association" of human beings all enjoying equal rights:

In place of the old bourgeois society, with its classes and class antagonisms, we shall have an association in which the free development of each is the condition for the free development of all. [57]

Unfortunately, Marx never expressed his thoughts on this issue any more precisely and concretely than this. He did not live to see the communist revolutions of the 20th Century. Consequently, it remains a matter of debate whether or not he would have been satisfied with the way that communism was put into practice in the Soviet Union, the German Democratic Republic and the other states forming the "socialist bloc" during the Cold War. But there is no denying that the 20th-Century communist states in general showed little progress toward abolishing the state as an instrument of domination, or (in Marx's own phrase) letting the state "wither away". On the contrary, what was seen in the communist states was most often rather an especially vast and rigid apparatus of state administration which tended to encourage the emergence of a new system of domination involving secret services and privileges for the new class of state functionaries and bureaucrats. There is, indeed, no conclusive answer to just how Marx envisaged, in detail, the "free development of all" within the new "associative" form of human political co-existence. But it may safely be assumed that a critical spirit and a humanist like Marx would not have given his approbation to the rigidly dogmatic, and often brutal, way in which communism was generally put into practice in the decades following the Russian Revolution.

Alienation

One idea of Marx's that remains very relevant still today is his critique of what he calls the "alienation" of labour in industrial society as it exists under capitalism.

By this term "alienation" Marx really means something very simple. The things that we make in our everyday work tend to become "strange" (or "alien") to us. Indeed, even the way we make them is unnatural. A worker, for example, in a capacitor factory who stands all day on a production line and performs, over and over, the same two motions but never gets to see the finished product that these motions contribute to creating – indeed possibly never even knows how the finished capacitors are later used – is someone who has lost all real relation to his work and to his own creative activity.

Such a worker is only selling his labour-power, while the product that this labour creates remains something completely alien to him. It is only the capitalist entrepreneur who knows whom the capacitors are sold to and in which radio sets they are finally installed.

Marx and Engels see alienation as a problem specifically of the modern era. People of early historical and pre-historic periods – whether hunters, gatherers or farmers – did not yet suffer from this problem. "They knew what became of their product," writes Engels. "They consumed it. It did not leave their hands. And as long as production was carried on on this basis it could not grow beyond the control of the producers and it could not conjure up any alien phantom powers against them, as is the case regularly and inevitably under civilization." [58]

As late as the Middle Ages there was still such a thing as non-alienated labour in which the worker could "find himself" in the product of his work. A saddler, for example, still made, in this era, the whole saddle by hand, decorated it with various designs and with his own personal initials, and proudly handed it over to his customer. He also set the price for his efforts himself. His work – that is to say, his saddles – were a part of himself, a part of his life, his own self-realization. He was proud of them.

The modern, wage-dependent factory- or office-worker, regardless of whether he is processing data on a computer or sitting on a production line, has no influence at all on the finished product. It belongs to him in no sense. This is why his work seems to him to be something burdensome and alien:

> Its alien character emerges clearly in the fact that as soon as no physical or other compulsion exists labour is shunned like the plague. [59]

This often leads to something like a split personality in modern Man. He finds no self-realization in his work but only in his leisure time and looks forward to his brief holidays as a way of recovering a sense of being alive:

> The worker, therefore, only feels himself outside his work and in his work feels outside himself. [...] His labour, therefore, is not voluntary but coerced; it is *forced labour*. [60]

Ending Alienation

These analyses of Marx's were made over one hundred and fifty years ago but are, sadly, still relevant today. Still today many people live only for their brief holiday periods and, during their working hours, feel like controlled and directed ants who are selling their lives away hour by hour. All the more exciting, then, is the solution that Marx and Engels propose. If we want to live once again in a natural, non-"alienated" way there is only one way to do so: "The old mode of production must be revolutionized from top to bottom, and in particular the former division of labour must disappear. Its place must be taken by an organization of production in which, on the one hand, no individual can throw on the shoulders of others his share in productive labour [...] and in which, on the other hand, productive labour, instead of being a means of subjugating men, will become a means of their emancipation [...]" [61]

Any such non-alienated mode of production must be organized without private property. Because it is private property alone that allows someone to "throw his share in labour onto the shoulders of others" and to live just from rent, interest, income from stocks and shares, or from the labour of his employees. The mode of production based on an economy of private property, then, must be replaced by one based on common, social property. The abolition of "wage-slavery", argues Engels, will lead to a great liberation. Inasmuch as work offers to "each individual the opportunity to develop all his faculties, physical and mental, in all directions and exercise them to the full", labour will become "a pleasure instead of being a burden". [62]

That labour, in a true communist society, will no longer be experienced as a burden results from the facts that, in such a society, each human being will be able to develop in a way concordant with his or her own special faculties and will also know that he or she is working not for the benefit of individual capitalists but for the good of society as a whole, in whose ownership all means of production henceforth stand.

The Realm of Freedom

Marx concedes, however, that even under communism there will be production lines and monotonous work, since such things are necessary for the manufacture of foodstuffs, tools and other basic items. Because however well and collectively organized social labour may be, work belongs by its nature to "the realm of necessity":

> Beyond it begins that development of human energy which is an end in itself, the true realm of freedom, which, however, can blossom forth only with this realm of necessity as its basis. [63]

Although, then, for Marx, we will remain forever dependent upon the necessity of work as the basis of our material social reproduction and self-expression, a progressive liberation from this necessity of work must remain a goal for society's further development:

Marx's Central Idea

> In fact, the realm of freedom actually begins only where labour which is determined by necessity and mundane considerations ceases. [64]

It was, then, Marx's great hope that by means of "rational production" and the targeted application of technology and machinery more and more people could be partially or entirely relieved of the necessity of labour, so that they could devote themselves rather to science, art and culture:

> The reduction of the working day is the basic prerequisite. [65]

The "realm of necessity", that is to say, is in the end just a staging post on the way to freedom.

Of What Use Is Marx's Discovery for Us Today?

Beware of the Sorceror – How Can Man Maintain Control?

Even after more than one hundred and fifty years, Marx's critique of the central mechanisms of capitalism remains astonishingly applicable today. "Larger capitals beat smaller", wrote Marx. Nowadays barely a day goes by without some smaller firm being bought up, taken over, or annihilated by a much larger one. Not even the introduction of anti-trust laws and corresponding supervisory bodies has been able to prevent the formation of monopolies and the practice of price-rigging. But it is not just the capital concentration described by Marx that is increasing all over the world; immiseration is increasing too. Thus, most industrialized nations have seen in recent years a great increase both in those situated at the very highest end of the earnings scale and in those scraping by at its lowest end on welfare payments or irregular low-paid work. Marx predicted that just such dramatic increases in the wealth gap would result from the capitalist economy:

There can be no doubt, then, but that Marx's critique of the market economy is still relevant. But of what concrete use is this critique for us today? What exactly can we improve in our economies? With reference to its enormous production of goods and its unmasterable financial system, Marx compares bourgeois capitalism with a sorcerer whose own magic has gotten out of his control:

> [...] Modern bourgeois society, [...] that has conjured up such gigantic means of production and exchange, is like the sorcerer who is no longer able to control the powers of the nether world whom he has called up by his spells. [67]

This analogy of the "sorcerer" is of especial relevance today because citizens of all nations do indeed find themselves increasingly helpless in the face of global financial crises.

The last great global financial crisis of 2008, for example, struck the world's population like an evil spell, without anyone seeming really to have been at fault. Politicians blamed the banks that proved insolvent due to rash speculations and unpaid loans. The bank managers blamed the customers who had failed to keep up with their mortgage payments. The customers blamed their low incomes which had made them unable to pay. Some banks also blamed the greed of their customers who had expected excessively high rates of interest on their savings accounts, so that the bank managers in their turn had been forced

Of What Use Is Marx's Discovery for Us Today?

into risky speculations. Smaller savers, but sometimes also larger investors, often place their money with the bank offering the highest interest rates and thereby the most profitable (but also the most speculative and risky) investments. And thus the pursuit of profit and speculation drive each other on to greater and greater extremes – as if set in motion by some sorcerer who can no longer control his own spell.

The sober analyses of financial experts basically conclude that what necessarily creates global financial crises are the high expectations as regards profits and benefits that are considered quite normal in capitalism and are shared by all economic actors, be they customers of banks or these banks managers and shareholders, or shareholders in companies. But these very expectations of profit form the motor of all productive forces in bourgeois capitalist society and are thereby sacrosanct. What, then, can be done in order to avoid future crises? According to Marx and Engels, there is only one real solution: "[...] When once their nature is understood, (these productive forces) can, in the hands of the producers working together, be transformed from master demons into willing servants. [...] With this recognition at last of the real nature of the productive forces of today, the social anarchy of production gives place to a social regulation of production upon a definite plan, according to the needs of the community and of each individual." [68]

This planned administration of production is, then, for Marx and Engels, the only solution to the problem of a capitalist production and speculation that would otherwise be uncontrollable. Such planning is synonymous with a communist takeover of all companies and banks, that is to say, the state control of all production processes. But the history of the socialist countries showed that the planned economy that Marx and Engels demanded also brought great problems. In these countries goods were often not produced in sufficient number or quality. Bottlenecks led to notoriously long queues at the shops. State planners and bureaucrats were very slow in reacting to the changing needs of the population and, in the end, it was the citizens themselves who turned their backs on the planned economy and overthrew communism. Since the dissolution of the former "socialist bloc" around 1990 we face the problem that, whereas Marx's criticisms of capitalism have proven, in many respects, valid, his proposed solution – the abolition of private property – is now known itself to be flawed.

But we can still learn something decisive from Marx.

We need to work hard to ensure that capitalism does not shake off all regulation. Because if society loses all control over the economy, then it really is lost. But control of the economy means a targeted, even if only limited, restriction of the free market. This is why so many countries have, since World War Two, supplemented and restricted market forces by drawing key services and industries under partial collective – i.e. state – control. Attempts have been made to "give capitalism a human face" by providing all citizens with a certain protection from poverty in the form of welfare, free education and free health care. Redistributive taxation systems were also introduced in order to reduce the danger of immiseration and replace the extremes of rich and poor with a "middle class" comprising most of society.

Many of these post-war achievements have, indeed, been wiped out by globalization and the growing competition with low-wage countries. In most European countries in 2016 education is no longer free, the quality of health care has (through the emergence of private health-insurance systems) once again become income-dependent, and the number of the very poor has begun to rise dramatically. Determined measures need to be taken against this.

If neither an unrestricted free market nor a totally

planned economy are goals worth striving for, a middle way must be found: one which allows the free unfolding of the individual's personal interests and desire for profit but limits this unfolding of individual aspirations where they negatively affect the dignity of others. The great task for the future, then, will be to find a way to allow self-interest while restricting human greed. Because it is unrestricted greed, in the end, that is the "sorcerer" that Marx quite rightly warned against. A society that loses control over its economy is lost. And to maintain control must mean, concretely, to create firm legal foundations for an efficient supervision of banks and private companies which will ensure that limits are set to the drive for profits.

Every Era Has Its Ideology, Even Our Own – The "Critique of Ideology" Today

Another discovery of Marx's that surely remains of great value is the connection between base and superstructure. Marx was the first to recognize the economic foundations of the whole of human social existence and the influence of these foundations also on cultural and intellectual development. And indeed there surely does exist a close connection between the way people secure their material survival and their convictions and beliefs. Even Marx's opponents have had to recognize this and, since Marx, just about every philosopher has tended to take material conditions into account when philosophizing.

It is certainly important for every human being to become aware of his or her economic base and thereby to gain a clear view of the mental superstructure that rests upon it. Just as the feudal system lent itself legitimacy through the idea of "the divine right of kings", the ideas of patriotism and nationalism were key legitimating factors for the bourgeois capitalist society of the 19th and 20th Centuries. Because pride in a shared language and ethnic origin bound the capitalist together with the wage-worker into a national community to which both could feel they belonged even despite their mutually antagonistic material interests. Marx critiqued this element of the superstructure as, from the viewpoint of the workers, mere "ideology", or "false consciousness"; he considered nationalism to be an idea which, in the end, served only the owners of land and capital:

Marx believed, then, that nationalism (which was a rising force in his lifetime) was a very dangerous ideology which the bourgeoisie was using to play off the workers in one country against the workers in others. When a worker goes to war, he argued, ostensibly in order to "defend his country", he is in fact not risking his life for his own interest but only for that of the possessors of land and means of production. Even if the war is one his country wins, the worker will gain no benefit from the victory. He will return to the job he had done before serving as a soldier and remain the "wage-slave" he was before. Why, then, should such a man fight for interests that are not his own? Never again, declared Marx, should a German worker fire upon a French or upon an English worker. It was in this spirit that he founded a trans-national federation of workers' parties – the so-called "International" – and ended his and Engels's famous *Communist Manifesto* with an appeal to the world's workers to no longer let themselves be played off against one another:

Marx would have been horrified if he had lived to experience how, despite his warning, two terrible world wars did indeed ensue in which German, French and English workers, as well as those of many other nations, shot each other down by the millions.

Today, the ideology of nationalism seems to have been overcome in almost all European countries. But if Marx was right and every society has its own "ruling ideology" which is a reflection and a legitimation of the respectively prevailing relations of production, then we must necessarily ask the question: what is the ruling ideology of our society? Does contemporary capitalism also have an ideology which legitimates the present economic system with its huge differences in income? Can we identify an intellectual superstructure of the present day which, even in the face of all our financial crises, tries to prove that the egoism of profit-seeking individuals is the natural destiny of human beings?

One does not need to look far for such an ideology. Our bookshops are full of publications that propound just such ideas as these and that, instead of critically analyzing and trying to improve our economic system, attempt to indisputably justify it as the sole true human condition. The British biologist Richard Dawkins, for example, wrote, some years ago, a book called The *Selfish Gene*, arguing that Man is genetically predetermined to be egoistic and to pursue selfish goals. Dawkins contests Darwin's classic thesis whereby evolution is a matter of the survival of the species, arguing that evolution rather obeys the law of the selfish propagation of one's own specific gene. Thus, he says, the first action of a young lion who drives off an old one and takes his place as head of a pride is to kill all the pride's newborns. This hastens the propagation of the young lion's genes because lionesses remain infertile until their offspring reach a certain age. Clearing the field for their immediate re-impregnation by killing all the young is, indeed, disadvantageous to the species; but it is advantageous to the propagation of the young lion's own "selfish gene". This example, says Dawkins, shows that the real aim of evolution is not, as Darwin had argued, the survival of the species but rather the egoism of the gene.

One cannot help but suspect, when reading such natural-scientific hypotheses, that we are dealing here less with really established truths than with an ideological superstructure in Marx's sense – that is to say, with "false consciousness". Dawkins's example of the selfish behaviour of the young lion may be valid; but many counter-examples to this can surely also be found in Nature. Elephants and buffalo, for instance, still raise newborns within the herd even if their mother dies. To point to specific examples within Nature, then, is extremely questionable in principle; one cannot simply present marriage as the only natural way of life because storks happen to live monogamously. There are just as many counter-examples and it would be arbitrary and self-deluding to model one's behaviour in terms of sexual fidelity on such examples from the natural world or to cite them as moral examples. The socio-biologist proceeds just as arbitrarily when he uses the supposedly genetically-coded behaviour of animals to draw conclusions about Man's behaviour in society.

But what is most suspect is that – in a situation in which individuals, worldwide, have to compete for jobs and resources – some natural scientists feel moved to provide a superstructure of ideas corresponding to this economic base – i.e. a body of ideas which presents the economic "war of all against all" as something natural and anchored in biology. The danger in such ideological "biologisms" – which often stretch science beyond its limits – is that those who, before reading such books, had waited patiently and politely in supermarket queues may, afterward, begin to push and shove their way to the front. As our society becomes more intensely competitive, we will surely see ever more pseudo-scientific proofs that selfishness is innate in human beings.

But if one has read Marx one knows that it must be borne in mind that such ostensibly scientific studies are, for the most part, typical superstructural phenomena. That is, they are just reflections – in the case discussed a particularly crude reflection – of the present-day material economic base and in no way constitute scientific truth. If Marx is right that every era produces its superstructure and its ideology, this applies to our era too. We must, then, remain alert and should, perhaps, even make "the critique of ideology" a subject taught in school. A vibrant society requires constant self-criticism and constant work on improving its material conditions. Also regarding scientific theories, then, one must always ask: what is truth here and what is ideological superstructure serving to perpetuate the prevailing economic conditions? Marx has provided us with the tools to recognize ideology as false consciousness and to free ourselves from it.

Making the Realm of Freedom a Reality – Work is Just a Staging Post

Perhaps the most beautiful and most important prospect that Marx has bequeathed to us is his vision of "the realm of freedom". Like so many of Marx's ideas, this vision displays a convincing logic. Human beings have always had to work in order to make their living. But in the course of history they have produced better and better means of production. Perhaps one day, thanks to such sophisticated machines as robots or computers, we will find that our social production and reproduction has become so efficient that we will be able to leave the realm of necessity and of alienated labour completely behind us. Already in his own day Marx recognized the growing efficiency of modern means of production and called, therefore, for massive reductions in working hours:

> The actual wealth of society and the possibility of constantly expanding its reproduction process, therefore, do not depend upon the duration of surplus labour but upon its productivity and upon the more or less copious conditions of production under which it is performed. [71]

Marx, in other words, held that the wealth of our society is based not on the hours that we work but rather on the types of technology, machinery and energy applied in this work. The foodstuffs that it once took an entire farmstead, with 10 children, 8 maids and 20 farm hands equipped with scythes and haycarts, to produce can today be produced by a single farmer using his farm machinery. Indeed, we are already seeing the first cars rolling off the production lines that have been built without any direct human labour at all.

This means that many developed societies are far from needing the labouring contribution of all their citizens in order to sustain themselves. Almost every European country has its unemployed. We think of this as a negative thing – as a lack or loss of gainful employment – but this negative connotation obscures what is potentially gained here. Because is it not a good thing, really, that thanks to machines and computers more and more people are being freed from mind-numbing, repetitive labour? Perhaps, then, we should speak of "freed" people rather than of "the unemployed". Marx was one of the first philosophers to point out that labour is not the only form of self-realization and that, in the future, large sections of the population may devote themselves entirely to the arts, the sciences, or research. He had the great vision of a realm of freedom beyond material labour:

If Marx is right and modern means of production will at some point allow us to free large sections of the population from labour altogether, then this prospect of self-development beyond material work must count as a laudable leap for humanity outside the "realm of necessity" – an historical milestone on mankind's path toward transcending a condition in which we live only to appropriate the substance of Nature. A related question here, of course, is the sharing-out of the continuing yield of social material production among those freed from personal involvement in this material production. For Marx it was clear that the non-labouring freed should get their share and this Marxist idea is in fact more and more discussed today under the form of the proposal of an "unconditional basic income".

The brilliance of this idea consists in the fact that every citizen receives this basic income even if he is also earning by his work. In this way, there is no cause for envy and everyone enjoys the freedom to increase his income and develop himself. But at the same time it is socially accepted that one may also live just from one's basic income and – as Marx so daringly prophetically envisaged – devote oneself rather to the sciences or the arts. In a world where there is, in any case, not enough work for all, it might even be considered laudable for an individual to choose this path involving less material reward but more possibilities for mental development. Moreover, such a system would dispense with the immense costs of staffing and administering the social security system, since this basic income would be paid out automatically, without the need for an application, to everyone from their eighteenth year on.

But regardless of what concrete solution is found, one thing is certain: modern society produces so efficiently that ever more people can indeed already be relieved of the necessity of work. Marx's vision, then, is already taking concrete form. Perhaps we have already arrived at that historical turning point which allows us to attempt something in this direction. Why not take the first step – into the "realm of freedom"?

Egoism May Bring Success – But Man Finds Completion Only as a "Species-Being"

To learn from Marx means to become aware of the roots of capitalism and to recognize its weaknesses. And its greatest weakness is surely at the same time its greatest strength: the egoism of the individual producer and consumer. Adam Smith, intellectual forefather of capitalism, once said that it was only due to such egoism that the supermarket shelves stay full. If a particular good becomes scarce, its price immediately rises and it produces a higher profit, with the result that other entrepreneurs begin to make this profitable product. Production of it increases until supply is in excess of demand and the manufacturers have to competitively lower their prices. In the end, the once-expensive product stands, low-priced and plentiful again, on the shelves. Adam Smith spoke,

Of What Use Is Marx's Discovery for Us Today?

somewhat euphorically, of this self-regulation of production as a "divine equilibrium" and also of an "invisible hand" which would convert the egoism of capitalist entrepreneurs into the general good.

The planned economies of the socialist states did indeed prove unable to match the speed and efficiency of the egoistically acting manufacturers and traders in Western Europe and the US. But this, the profit motive that so powerfully drives capitalism, was and remains its greatest weakness. As Engels wrote: "Naked greed has been the moving spirit of civilization from its first day to the present time. Wealth, wealth, and wealth again; wealth not of society but of this shabby individual was its sole determining aim." [73]

These words of admonishment are, sadly, still very relevant. Even today, wherever the market is not directly regulated by the state and its laws, greed and egoism cause great harm to society. In many spheres Smith's "invisible hand" does not work at all, as in the case of board members in large companies who award themselves salaries and bonuses which bear no relation to the work they actually contribute. The profit drive also takes a heavy toll on the environment. While bourgeois capitalist society, then, raises its citizens to be, in many respects, egoists who assert themselves as individuals in constant competition with other egoistic individuals, this form of socialization is, for Marx, one which misses the true path marked out for Man by his essential nature:

Man is a species-being [...]. 74

By this Marx means, firstly, that human beings are by nature not egoistic "loners" but rather social beings who live together in families, communities and states, and who mate, reproduce, work together and also eat and enjoy their leisure together. But secondly – and this is the deeper meaning of this claim – Marx means that it is only as a "species-being" that Man can find real satisfaction by fulfilling his essential destiny. Already as a very young man, in his high-school graduation essay, Marx had written:

But the chief guide that must direct us [...] is the welfare of mankind and our own perfection. It should not be thought that these two interests could be in conflict [...].

Of What Use Is Marx's Discovery for Us Today?

> On the contrary, Man's nature is so constituted that he can attain his own perfection only by working for the perfection, the good, of his fellow men. [75]

One is, of course, always strongly tempted to be guided by one's own interests and to apply all one's energy to ensuring one's own and one's family's wellbeing. But human life is not just about improving one's own and one's family's lot but also about making society as a whole more worth living in. Dedication to others; the feeling of responsibility for society as a whole; in short, a readiness to stand up for the welfare of all – this, for Marx, is the true, and perhaps the highest, calling and destiny of Man:

> If he works only for himself, he may perhaps become a famous man of learning, a great sage, an excellent poet, but he can never be a perfect, truly great man. [76]

Bibliographical References:

1. Karl Marx and Friedrich Engels, Collected Works, Lawrence and Wishart Ltd. London, 1975, Vol. 6, p. 482 ("Manifesto of the Communist Party")
2. Karl Marx and Friedrich Engels, Collected Works, Lawrence and Wishart Ltd. London, 1975, Vol. 5, p. 5 ("Theses on Feuerbach")
3. Karl Marx and Friedrich Engels, Collected Works, Lawrence and Wishart Ltd. London, 1975, Vol. 6, p. 482 ("Manifesto of the Communist Party")
4. Karl Marx and Friedrich Engels, Collected Works, Lawrence and Wishart Ltd. London, 1975, Vol. 39, p. 181 (Letter, Marx to Engels, 8th of September, 1852)
5. Karl Marx and Friedrich Engels, Collected Works, Lawrence and Wishart Ltd.. London, 1975, Vol. 5, pps. 41-42 ("The German Ideology")
6. Ibid. p. 42
7. Karl Marx and Friedrich Engels, Grundrisse: Foundations for an Outline of the Critique of Political Economy (Rough Draft) translated by Martin Nicholas, Penguin Books, London, 1993, p. 87
8. Karl Marx and Friedrich Engels, Collected Works, Lawrence and Wishart Ltd. London, 1975, Vol. 5, p. 31 ("The German Ideology")
9. Karl Marx, Early Writings, Pelican Books, London, 1975, p. 328 ("Economic-Philosophical Manuscripts")
10. Karl Marx, Capital, Volume One, Penguin Books, London, 1976, p. 290
11. Karl Marx, Early Writings, Pelican Books, London, 1975, p. 329 ("Economic-Philosophical Manuscripts")
12. Ibid. pps. 328-29
13. Ibid.
14. Karl Marx and Friedrich Engels, Collected Works, Lawrence and Wishart, London, 1975, Vol. 5, p. 31 ("The German Ideology")
15. Ibid. pps. 31-32

16 Karl Marx and Friedrich Engels, Collected Works, Lawrence and Wishart Ltd. London, 1975, Vol. 5, p. 32, p. 37, ("The German Ideology")
17 Karl Marx, Early Writings, Pelican Books, London, 1975, p. 349 ("Economic and Philosophical Manuscripts")
18 Karl Marx and Friedrich Engels, Collected Works, Lawrence and Wishart Ltd. London, 1975, Vol. 25, p. 87 (Engels, Anti-Duehring)
19 Karl Marx and Friedrich Engels, Collected Works, Lawrence and Wishart Ltd. London, 1975, Vol. 5, p. 36 ("The German Ideology")
20 Ibid.
21 Karl Marx and Friedrich Engels, Collected Works, Lawrence and Wishart Ltd. London, 1975, Vol. 6, p. 503 ("Manifesto of the Communist Party")
22 Karl Marx, Early Writings, Pelican Books, London, 1975, p. 244 ("A Contribution to the Critique of Hegel's Philosophy of Right")
23 Ibid.
24 Ibid.
25 Ibid.
26 Ibid. 244-45
27 Ibid. p. 251
28 Karl Marx and Friedrich Engels, Collected Works, Lawrence and Wishart Ltd. London, 1975, Vol. 26, p. 273 (Engels, "The Origin of the Family, Private Property and the State")
29 Ibid.
30 Karl Marx and Friedrich Engels, Collected Works, Lawrence and Wishart Ltd. London, 1975, Vol. 6, p. 482 ("Manifesto of the Communist Party")
31 Ibid.
32 Ibid. p. 489
33 Ibid. p. 488
34 Ibid. p. 489
35 Karl Marx and Friedrich Engels, Collected Works, Lawrence and Wishart Ltd. London, 1975, Vol. 35, p. 751 ("Capital" Volume One)

36 Karl Marx and Friedrich Engels, Collected Works,
    Lawrence and Wishart Ltd. London, 1975, Vol. 6, p. 519
    ("Manifesto of the Communist Party")
37 Karl Marx and Friedrich Engels, Collected Works,
    Lawrence and Wishart Ltd. London, 1975, Vol. 9, p. 213
    (Marx and Engels, "Wage Labour and Capital")
38 Ibid. p. 214
39 Karl Marx and Friedrich Engels, Collected Works,
    Lawrence and Wishart Ltd. London, 1975, Vol. 9, p. 202
    (Marx and Engels, "Wage Labour and Capital")
40 Karl Marx and Friedrich Engels, Collected Works,
    Lawrence and Wishart Ltd. London, 1975, Vol. 35, p. 614
    ("Capital" Volume One)
41 Ibid. p. 621
42 Ibid.
43 Ibid.
44 Ibid. p. 621-22
45 Ibid. p. 750
46 Ibid. p. 621
47 Ibid. p. 750
48 Ibid. p. 638
49 Karl Marx and Friedrich Engels, Collected Works,
    Lawrence and Wishart Ltd. London, 1975, Vol. 29, p. 263
    ("Preface to a Contribution to the Critique of Political Economy")
50 Karl Marx and Friedrich Engels, Collected Works,
    Lawrence and Wishart Ltd. London, 1975, Vol. 35, p. 750
    ("Capital" Volume One)
51 Karl Marx and Friedrich Engels, Collected Works,
    Lawrence and Wishart Ltd. London, 1975, Vol. 5, p. 49
    ("German Ideology")
52 Karl Marx and Friedrich Engels, Collected Works,
    Lawrence and Wishart Ltd. London, 1975, Vol. 6, p. 498
    ("Manifesto of the Communist Party")
53 Karl Marx, Early Writings, Pelican Books, London, 1975, p. 251
    ("A Contribution to the Critique of Hegel's Philosophy of Right")
54 Karl Marx and Friedrich Engels, Collected Works,
    Lawrence and Wishart Ltd. London, 1975, Vol. 5, pps. 52-3
    ("German Ideology")

55   Ibid. p. 53
56   Karl Marx and Friedrich Engels, Collected Works, Lawrence and Wishart Ltd. London, 1975, Vol. 29, p. 263 ("Preface to a Contribution to the Critique of Political Economy")
57   Karl Marx and Friedrich Engels, Collected Works, Lawrence and Wishart Ltd. London, 1975, Vol. 6, p. 506 ("Manifesto of the Communist Party")
58   Karl Marx and Friedrich Engels, Collected Works, Lawrence and Wishart Ltd. London, 1975, Vol. 26, p. 273 (Engels, "Origin of the Family, Private Property and the State")
59   Karl Marx, Early Writings, Pelican Books, London, 1975, p. 326 ("Economic and Philosophical Manuscripts")
60   Ibid.
61   Karl Marx and Friedrich Engels, Collected Works, Lawrence and Wishart Ltd. London, 1975, Vol. 25, p. 280 (Engels, "Anti-Duehring")
62   Ibid.
63   Karl Marx and Friedrich Engels, Collected Works, Lawrence and Wishart Ltd. London, 1975, Vol. 37, p. 807 ("Capital, Volume Three")
64   Ibid.
65   Ibid.
66   Karl Marx and Friedrich Engels, Collected Works, Lawrence and Wishart Ltd. London, 1975, Vol. 35, p. 621 ("Capital" Volume One)
67   Karl Marx and Friedrich Engels, Collected Works, Lawrence and Wishart Ltd. London, 1975, Vol. 6, p. 489 ("Manifesto of the Communist Party")
68   Karl Marx and Friedrich Engels, Collected Works, Lawrence and Wishart Ltd. London, 1975, Vol. 24, p. 320 (Engels, "Socialism: Utopian and Scientific")
69   Karl Marx and Friedrich Engels, Collected Works, Lawrence and Wishart Ltd. London, 1975, Vol. 6, p. 503 ("Manifesto of the Communist Party")
70   Ibid. p. 519
71   Karl Marx and Friedrich Engels, Collected Works, Lawrence and Wishart Ltd. London, 1975, Vol. 37, p. 807 ("Capital, Volume Three")

72 Ibid.
73 Karl Marx and Friedrich Engels, Collected Works, Lawrence and Wishart Ltd. London, 1975, Vol. 26, p. 275 (Engels, "Origin of the Family, Private Property and the State")
74 Karl Marx, Early Writings, Pelican Books, London, 1975, p. 327 ("Economic and Philosophical Manuscripts")
75 Karl Marx and Friedrich Engels, Collected Works, Lawrence and Wishart Ltd. London, 1975, Vol. 1, p. 8 (Karl Marx, school essay, "Reflections of a Young Man on the Choice of a Profession")
76 Ibid.

Already published in the same series:

Walther Ziegler
Camus in 60 Minutes
ISBN 9783741227738

Walther Ziegler
Freud in 60 Minutes
ISBN 9783741227707

Walther Ziegler
Hegel in 60 Minutes
ISBN 9783741227677

Walther Ziegler
Heidegger in 60 Minutes
ISBN 9783741227752

Walther Ziegler
Kant in 60 Minutes
ISBN 9783741226373

Walther Ziegler
Marx in 60 Minutes
ISBN 9783741227691

Walther Ziegler
Platon in 60 Minutes
ISBN 9783741227615

Walther Ziegler
Rousseau in 60 Minutes
ISBN 9783741227622

Walther Ziegler
Sartre in 60 Minutes
ISBN 9783741227653

Walther Ziegler
Smith in 60 Minutes
ISBN 9783741227721

Coming soon in the same series:

Walther Ziegler
Adorno in 60 Minutes

Walther Ziegler
Arendt in 60 Minutes

Walther Ziegler
Bacon in 60 Minutes

Walther Ziegler
Descartes in 60 Minutes

Walther Ziegler
Foucault in 60 Minutes

Walther Ziegler
Habermas in 60 Minutes

Walther Ziegler
Hobbes in 60 Minutes

Walther Ziegler
Nietzsche in 60 Minutes

Walther Ziegler
Popper in 60 Minutes

Walther Ziegler
Rawls in 60 Minutes

Walther Ziegler
Schopenhauer in 60 Minutes

Walther Ziegler
Wittgenstein in 60 Minutes

The author:

Dr Walther Ziegler is academically trained in the fields of philosophy, history and political science. As a foreign correspondent, reporter and newsroom coordinator for the German TV station ProSieben he has produced films on every continent. His news reports have won several prizes and awards. He has also authored numerous books in the field of philosophy. His many years of experience as a journalist mean that he is able to present the complex ideas of the great philosophers in a way that is both engaging and very clear. Since 2007 he has also been active as a teacher and trainer of young TV journalists in Munich, holding the post of Academic Director at the Media Academy, an institute of higher education that offers film and TV courses at its base directly on the site of the major European film production company Bavaria Film.